M000211863

HELP! THERE'S A JUDAS ON MY JOB!

9 Steps For Surviving Workplace Betrayal

Kanisha L. Adkins

Foreword by Rev. John W. Kinney PhD

3E Publishing
Glen Allen

Karen:
Miracles, Peace,
and Blessings,
Kamala Harris

This Book Is Dedicated To

Marquia (my niece), Michael (my nephew),
the Millennial Generation,
and those who will come after them.
I wish you great success in your professions and
throughout your lives.

CONTENTS

ACKNOWLEDGEMENTS

Daddy (Rufus), Mama (Carleen), Selina, Marquia and Michael, thank you for loving who I am and admiring what I do. There *is* a difference and I'm glad you know the difference. Throughout my periods of unemployment, and my job woes, you never judged *me* as problematic or "less than". Instead, you loved me even more, through your words, and your actions. Vincent Jones, Shirley Knox and Mildred Best, my former co-workers but more importantly my "forever friends", thank you for keeping me sane, focused, grounded and, when necessary, distracted, while I was at work with my Judas. Tounya C. Wright, my neighbor and friend, thank you for giving me a shoulder to cry on while I was home. You were dealing with your own Judas on your job, so you understood *exactly* what I was going through. Thank God you lived right around the corner! Willy Ann Davis and the 2003-2004 second grade class of Blandford Elementary School in Petersburg, Virginia, thank you for the love, the hugs, and the laughs, and for allowing the teacher in me to use her gifts. The school's doors are closed now but you gave me what I needed when I needed it most.

Frank Crawley and Littycia Clay-Crawley, my partners in ministry, my travel buddies, and my foodie friends, thank you for giving me a book on publishing. I know you thought I'd never use it but "to everything there is a season." I promise you, I read it immediately, and have referred to it frequently. *Now* is the season for the fruit of your gift, which has been and is priceless. T. L. Prince, thank you for your feedback as a human resources professional. Galaxy Systems Corporations, thank you for an excellent editorial experience and for encouraging me to stay away from clichés and to stay in my own voice.

Wyvetra Brown (hair stylist), and Anita Hill-Moses (owner of Braids and Dreds Natural Hair Salon, Inc., Richmond, Virginia), many, many thanks to you, for styling my hair for the photo shoot and for always keeping my hair professional and "on point". Clifton Gunn Photography, thank you for an *amazing* and fun photo shoot, and an *awesome* photo for my book cover. I look forward to working with you again in the future. Syreeta Bailey Stewart, Esquire, thank you for giving me access to the perfect setting for my photo shoot. LaRhonda Carter, thank you for encouraging me and reminding me to celebrate *every* step of the book-writing, publishing and marketing process, and not just the finished product. You entered my journey long after the events that caused me to write this book. But you assumed the position of cheerleader, and what a cheerleader you were! Alexis Harris, thank you for walking with me through my valleys, shouting with me on my mountain tops, believing with me and for me that God has a plan and a purpose for my life, and reminding me that greater was coming. Thank you "good buddy." John W. Kinney, (who I also call Reverend Doctor Dean), words don't adequately express the gratefulness I feel that a man of your stature would find my story worthy to carry your name. Thank you for your time, guidance and generosity, and for regarding this as "a good work."

Last but not least, a big THANK YOU to God, the Creator, for moving me to a deeper level of maturity, for motivating me to tap into my creative energy in order to heal my hurt and, for giving me the fuel I needed to be better and to help others. Judas meant it for evil but God used it for good. To God Be the Glory! Great Things God Has Done!

FOREWORD

One of the things I appreciate about the sacred text communicating the narrative around the life of Jesus is that it does not roseate reality. In the narrative, we discover that in the inner circle of leadership of the nascent Christian community there was at least one who betrayed Jesus and the mission of the movement. Could this aspect of the story be included as a stark reminder that even among competent and committed teams there will be deceptive and self-serving individuals? These individuals, though often quite capable, have a "hole in the soul" that shrinks behavior to the personal and the petty, and weaves a web of deception that wounds persons and pollutes practices.

The Rev. Kanisha L. Adkins, with refreshing honesty and transparency, shares her own experience with workplace betrayal. As her soul speaks, you can feel her pain, but her testimony is not about pain. Her work offers constructive practices that can strip betrayal of its power and alter its intent. Rev. Adkins' story and suggestive steps for engaging betrayal and betrayers is not intended to be exhaustive or final. What is provided is a substantive reflection that guides us to recognize and respond to betrayal in a fashion that moves us from pain to promise. In the end, betrayal cannot determine your person or your practice; your worth or your work.

As we move from "paying attention" to "saying our prayers," Rev. Adkins reminds us that the future is neither controlled nor defined by betrayers. "Run on see what the end is going to be!"

--John W. Kinney--
Samuel DeWitt Proctor, School of Theology,
Virginia Union University
Ebenezer Baptist Church, Beaverdam, Virginia

INTRODUCTION

E veryday at work, people are finding themselves in the position of having to deal with backstabbing and betrayal by the very people whom they thought they could trust. It doesn't matter whether you work in a hair salon, a courtroom, a hospital or a hotel. It doesn't matter whether you're paid hundreds of thousands of dollars a year by a major corporation or whether you volunteer to serve in a ministry at your local church. Betrayal and backstabbing on the job are real, and it can be ruthless.

Maybe you're one of those people, trying to come to terms with the fact that the person who flashed the brightest smile at you also had a sharp knife waiting to stab you in your back. If you're dealing with the problem of betrayal on your job, you're in good company. Betrayal isn't new. Some very famous and influential people throughout history also had this same problem.

In elementary school history classes you learned about Benedict Arnold who betrayed George Washington during the American Revolutionary War with England. And you may have learned in high school about Brutus who betrayed

Julius Caesar. But, probably, the most famous person to ever be betrayed was Jesus Christ. Public schools definitely didn't teach you about him! No, more than likely, you had to be seated on a pew in someone's church to learn about this man.

But what did you learn? You probably learned a lot. But did you learn how to survive betrayal? Probably not! At most, you were taught to be forgiving. To turn the other cheek. To turn it over to Jesus. To *let go and let God.* All of these admonitions are great end results. But how do you get to the end results? How do you get to the end result of forgiving and turning the other cheek? How do you get to the end result of turning it over to Jesus and letting go and letting God? Let's be honest. Betrayal isn't a lesson that usually comes up in Sunday school or Bible study. And when it does come up, it's usually once a year when it's time to turn your attention to the Passion of Christ and the Crucifixion. But after you've celebrated the resurrection of your Savior on Sunday, you have to walk back into your job on Monday, carrying your own personal cross, struggling and trying to figure out how to deal with your Judas.

It's time to stop struggling! If you want to know how to handle *your* Judas, look at how Jesus handled *His* Judas. Look and Learn! Even Jesus had to deal with on-the-job betrayal. We don't usually think of Jesus as having a job and co-workers. But maybe we should! Jesus and the twelve disciples worked together to feed the hungry, heal the sick, raise the dead, make lepers clean, and drive out demons. They spent sunny days and cloudy days together. Their time together wasn't simply for rest and relaxation. It was in an effort to accomplish specific tasks and goals. They had a mission and a vision. They worked under the pressure of deadlines and guidelines. They had places to go, people to meet and things to do.

Jesus had a job. Jesus had co-workers. And Jesus had Judas, the co-worker who betrayed Him. So, if God's son, Jesus, had to work with a backstabber, more than likely, at some point in life, whether it's for an extended period of time or a brief period of time, you'll have to work with a Judas too!

In 2000, after being hired for what I thought would be a dream job, I came face to face with my own personal 'Judas on the Job'. For three years, I struggled! I struggled to do the job I was hired to do. I struggled to do my job without allowing the backstabbing antics of my Judas to distract me from producing the high quality of work I knew I was capable of producing. I struggled to understand why I was being targeted. I struggled to find out exactly 'who' was targeting me. I struggled to hold onto my sanity, and my peace of mind. And I struggled to get up, get out, and get on with life.

And after my employment on that job ended, I struggled to shake off the hurt, and the pain that I had experienced, and unconsciously carried for the next year or two, even into the next job. Looking back, I have no doubt that the defensiveness I displayed, and the defenses I wore in subsequent situations on new jobs, were the result of unresolved pain inflicted by my Judas.

I was a licensed attorney and proficient in my profession. I was *Reverend* Kanisha L. Adkins, duly licensed and ordained, seasoned in my faith, and experienced in ministry. And yet, none of this excused me from the sting of being stabbed in the back by a co-worker, whom I thought was trustworthy. Instead, I was challenged to take all that I had, all that I knew, and all that I was, and to use it to get beyond the betrayal. I needed a model of how to survive and how to thrive. I found that model in a sacred text.

A close look at the relationship between Jesus and Judas, as told in the New Testament gospel of Matthew, holds some helpful hints on how to minimize the impact of betrayal. More importantly, if you're not able to leave the job, if you still need an income, and if you're willing to put forth some effort and follow the steps presented in this book, it's possible for you to not only minimize the effects of the betrayal - you can actually be better, in spite of it!

PAY ATTENTION

━━‡‡━━

*As he walked by the Sea of Galilee, he saw two
brothers, Simon, who is called Peter, and Andrew
his brother, casting a net into the sea – for they were
fishermen. And he said to them, "Follow me, and I
will make you fish for people." Immediately they left
their nets and followed him. As he went from there,
he saw two other brothers, James son of Zebedee
and his brother John, in the boat with their father
Zebedee, mending their nets, and he called them.*

(New Revised Standard Version Matthew 4:18-21)

*These are the names of the twelve apostles:
first, Simon, also known as Peter, and his
brother Andrew; James, son of Zebedee, and his
brother John; Philip and Bartholomew; Thomas*

1

and Matthew, the tax collector; James, son of Alphaeus, and Thaddaeus; Simon the Canaanite, and Judas Iscariot, the one who betrayed him.

(Matthew 10:2-4)

━✢ ✢━

How to Recognize Judas

Working with people for most of your waking hours can be hard work! And if it's difficult for *you* to meet deadlines and accomplish goals, all while trying to navigate and cope with your co-workers' various personalities, why would you think it was an easy job for Jesus? Sure, Jesus was divine, but he was human, too. He had a job. He was an itinerant preacher. Calling his job a "ministry" didn't make it any easier, and it won't make yours any easier either. It doesn't matter what you call your job: call it a ministry, call it a corporation, call it a committee or call it a sole proprietorship. No matter what you call it, it's still work, and you'll still have to work with people. At some point, there will be bumps in the road. And one of those bumps might be a Judas.

Jesus' job as an itinerant preacher lasted about three years. He was about 30 years old when he started recruiting people to work with him. I know we like to think of Jesus as "calling" disciples. It sounds so much more spiritual. But thinking about it in terms of "recruitment" and "hiring" can help us understand that what Jesus was about to do was nothing short of a job! This was going to be work, and Jesus needed people to help him accomplish his mission. According to Matthew's version of the "calling" of the disciples, Simon Peter and Andrew were called at the same time. It also seems that James and John, the sons of Zebedee, were called at the same time. Aside from these four, it isn't clear when the other eight were called or the order in which they were called. But it seems that Jesus called them during the early part of those three years when he went from town to town preaching, teaching, healing and delivering.

The relationship that the disciples shared with Jesus was more than just a brief, casual relationship. They spent most, if not all, of Jesus' three years of preaching, with Him. They spent the inspired moments, when Jesus taught and performed miracles, and they spent the ordinary moments, when they sought to make it from one day to the next. They traveled the countryside. They ate meals together. And they probably experienced hunger together, too. They shared sleeping quarters, sailed over stormy seas and faced demons with Him. This group spent a lot of time with Jesus, and Judas was part of this group. Jesus spent time with Judas. That's how Jesus knew Judas.

Jesus and Judas worked together for almost three years. Judas wasn't some stranger that Jesus just bumped into on the streets of Galilee one day. They worked together. And while they worked together, Jesus paid attention to Judas' character and temperament. He listened to the things Judas said and He watched the things Judas did. Jesus could have spent those three years working with Judas and never suspected that Judas would betray Him. But during those three years, Jesus had been paying attention to everything and everyone around Him. Jesus paid attention and that's how He was able to identify Judas as someone who would betray Him. Some people might say that Jesus had the gift of discernment and that's how He knew Judas would betray him. Jesus did have the gift of discernment but that doesn't mean He wasn't paying attention. In fact, discernment doesn't work without paying attention. Without a doubt, discernment and paying attention go hand in hand. And it's this combination of discernment and paying attention that, I believe, helped Jesus identify Judas as a betrayer.

In the United States, people who work full-time generally work anywhere from 32 to 60 hours a week, and some work even more. That's a lot of time to spend with people who aren't your family members or part of your inner circle of friends. And not only do we spend a significant amount of time on the job with our co-workers, we spend "prime time" with our co-workers. In other words, we spend "quality time" with them, the most productive parts of our days.

Yes, you've been hired to show up for several hours a day and to do a particular job. But while you're doing the job you've been hired to do, there's something else you need to do. PAY ATTENTION! If you're paying attention, you'll discover that you know the co-worker or co-workers who may have the potential to be a Judas. This doesn't mean that you'll know exactly when you'll be betrayed. It also doesn't mean that you should walk around in a state of paranoia, thinking that everyone is out to get you. What it means, though, is that by paying attention, you can discover that your Judas is closer to you than you think. Pay attention because people will tell you who they are. People will tell you who they are by what they do and by what they don't do, by what they say and by what they don't say. Just Pay Attention!

Judas isn't a stranger. Judas isn't that person who you think of as a blatant, out-right enemy. No, Judas is a person who's close by, someone who appears to be very friendly, welcoming, and in your corner. In fact, that's how Judas is able to get to you. Judas gets up close and personal, trying to get on your good side. That's how Judas got to Jesus. He got up close and personal, close enough to kiss him. Judas is someone who looks like a team player. Judas looks like he or she is part of the group. But look a little closer and you'll notice that there's something slightly off, something a little askew. Judas almost blends in, but if you're paying attention, you'll notice the differences.

But differences by themselves aren't what make up Judas. People are different and shouldn't be blamed for being different. No one has to be a carbon copy of anyone else. Everyone is unique and different and has his and her own gifts and strong points. Everyone on the job brings his and her own individual piece of the puzzle. But there's something about Judas' piece of the puzzle that doesn't quite fit.

So pay attention to the different personalities and temperaments of the people around you at work. It's easy to notice the loud, talkative people. And it's easy to spot the quiet, timid ones. Either of them could be a Judas. But there are so many other people in between the loud and the timid. And more than likely, Judas is somewhere in the middle, trying to blend in. So pay attention! Pay attention to everything. Do you have co-workers who seem to want to speak their minds when it's just the two of you, but then they act as if they can't talk when certain other people are around? Or do you have co-workers who have one opinion around one group of people and another opinion around another group of people? Or perhaps you have co-workers who say one thing but do a different thing. You'd be surprised what you can learn about a person if you just pay attention.

Years ago, in the 1970's, the legendary R&B singer Teddy Pendergrass recorded a song titled, "If You Don't Know Me By Now." In the song, he talks about a man and a woman who have been in a relationship for years. Based on the length of the relationship, (that would be quantity), and based on all of the experiences they've shared (that would be quality), they should know each other's personality and character. They've been together long enough to know what the other will do and what the other won't do. But there's a problem. Even after all of this time, the man feels like the woman really doesn't know him. It sounds like she's been distracted and hasn't been paying attention, because if she *had* been paying attention, she would know him.

Pay attention! The person who has the potential to be your Judas on the job is a person with whom you spend a lot of time. And during this age of technology, spending time with people on the job includes time spent in person as well as time spent on the telephone, time spent sending emails and text messages, and time in video and audio conferences. When you look at it this way, you can see that people spend a tremendous amount of time at work and in working relationships. It's no wonder there are so many Judases on the job. And you don't have to go out of your way to recognize your Judas. You don't have to go out to lunch, take breaks, or have Judas to your house for dinner. He or she is right there in that office, Monday through Friday, between the hours of 9 a.m. and 5 p.m. (or whatever your work schedule might be). Your Judas is working with you, day in and day out. Forty hours a week (and maybe more) is a lot of time to spend with anyone. Since you're putting in the time, you need to pay attention. It's called multi-tasking. You do it all of the time. *Judas watching* is just one more item you should add to your *to-do* list.

Judas is someone with whom you spend time, not only quantity time but also quality time. Judas isn't the man or woman down the hall who you only occasionally see on the elevator or in the lunchroom. Judas isn't someone who walks into your place of business from the street one day to simply deliver a package. People are betrayed by those who are closest to them. Professional betrayal comes from people with whom you work closely.

My Judas turned out to be my Administrative Assistant. You can't get much closer in a working relationship than the person who reports directly to you. We worked in the same office, on the same projects, for at least eight hours each day. I had no idea that her goal was to get me fired. I never dreamed that she was feeding my supervisor bad press about me. But one thing I did know was that within just a few short months of when we started working together, her behavior and attitude toward me had changed. I noticed this difference because, in addition to doing my work, I was paying attention to everything. I paid attention to everyone with whom I worked. I paid attention to what they were hired to do and I paid attention to how they did what they were hired to do. I even went as far as to pay attention to how they interacted with other people, both professionally and casually. I paid attention to the language they used, to the tone with which they spoke, and to their body language. I knew my Administrative Assistant was up to no good because I paid attention.

And that's what you need to do. Pay attention to everything and everybody and when it comes to knowing *your* Judas, make sure you're not falling asleep on the job. If there's a Judas on your job and if you're paying attention, you can discover, long before the betrayal happens, that you already know who Judas might be.

This may sound like you're being paranoid. But that's not what I'm suggesting. The goal of paying attention is not for you to be paranoid but for you to be observant. And there is a difference between being paranoid and being observant. *Paranoid,* as defined by Dictionary.com, means "to be excessively suspicious of the actions or motives of other people without having a basis or reason for being suspicious." Dictionary.com also defines *observant,* as "being quick to notice and perceive, or to attentively watch things that are actually happening." When you're paranoid, you're only imagining that someone is doing or saying certain things. But when you're observant, you're noticing the things that people actually do and say.

People communicate in a variety of ways and not just through words. Body language and facial expressions can tell us just as much as words. And *how* we say things can often mean as much as *what* we say. Being observant will allow you to objectively learn about your co-workers. Being paranoid will cause you to make subjective and sometimes wrong assumptions about them. Remember, you want to be observant as you're getting to know your co-workers.

After you've gotten to know your co-workers, and particularly, after you discover you've been betrayed, you can easily become paranoid. That's why it's important that you follow the third step addressed in this book. Following *Step Three* will help you redirect your attention away from being consumed by Judas' behavior and back to focusing on more important things.

STEP 1
REMINDERS

- Judas is someone who has a close personal or professional relationship with you and someone whom you think is trustworthy.
- Judas may *appear* to be supportive, friendly, in your corner, and genuinely interested in you.
- Judas will change his or her behavior and opinions based on who's around and who's listening.

PAY ATTENTION!

STEP 2
DON'T TAKE IT PERSONALLY

≈⊹ ⊹≈

*Then one of the twelve, who was called Judas
Iscariot, went to the chief priests and said, "What
will you give me if I betray him to you?" They
paid him thirty pieces of silver. And from that
moment he began to look for an opportunity to
betray him.*

(Matthew 26:14-16)

≈⊹ ⊹≈

Understanding the Mind of Judas

In *Step One*, I told you to PAY ATTENTION! And, unfortunately but realistically, by paying attention, you may
have identified some people who might betray or have already betrayed your trust. Now that you're paying attention

and you've identified "who," you might find yourself trying to figure out "why." In other words, you might want to know why this person with whom you worked so closely, this person with whom you thought you shared common goals, would want to stab you in the back and sabotage you.

You need to understand that betrayal is always motivated by something. We think that people backstab and betray in order to get something tangible in return, and that the beginning of betrayal is the hope of what they'll earn in the end. This is, in fact, what the Bible suggests about why Judas betrayed Jesus.

The gospel of Matthew paints a picture of a man who was motivated by money. Money may have been what Judas received after betraying Jesus, but money wasn't the motivation. In fact, what is earned in the end is never the motivation for anyone who betrays other people's trust. The motivation for betrayal starts long before the act of betrayal. The motivation is not about what they can get. It's about what they don't have. The motivation of people who engage in betrayal grows out of their feelings of deficiency. But the deficiency isn't that they feel they don't have enough money or some other tangible possession. The deficiency is that they are unfulfilled. In other words, the deficiency isn't in not *having* enough. The deficiency is in not *being* enough. And more than likely, the betrayer isn't even aware of these feelings.

I know you may not have time to do a psychological work-up on the first day you meet Judas on your job. But if you know the "why," you may be able to handle the 'who". Hopefully you can deal with your Judas a little bit better if you understand that 'hurt people' hurt people. You really need to wrap your brain around that concept. People who live in pain have the propensity to look for somewhere else to put their pain. And for people whose pain is emotional and who feel like they aren't enough, that somewhere else can often be other people.

When we look at Judas Iscariot in the Bible, we're told very little about him. The writer, John, mentions that Judas was in charge of the money. In other words, he was the treasurer and/or financial secretary. Matthew, however, doesn't address Judas' job in Jesus' organization of disciples. The gospel writer Matthew mentions Judas Iscariot three times, each time lifting up his role in the betrayal of Jesus. We're not told what his occupation was before Jesus selected him to be a disciple. We're not told that Judas was from Kerioth (also known as Carioth), in the lower part of Judah, unlike the other eleven disciples who were from Galilee in the Northern part of Israel. We can only speculate that Judas may have felt like an outsider because he was from somewhere else. We can only speculate that long before Judas met Jesus and the other eleven disciples, something happened in his life to create feelings of deficiency in him, something that made him feel as if he wasn't good enough. And maybe Judas tried to fill the emptiness in his soul by filling his pockets with thirty pieces of silver. But he soon found out that even the money wasn't enough to fill the emptiness he felt on the inside.

Judases sell out co-workers in order to get their own personal pay-offs. The pay-off may be something tangible, but often the pay-off is something intangible, like the approval of a person in authority, or popularity with a certain group of people. The outward pay-off is simply a way to erase or ease an internal deficiency. And while the Judases of the world have their eyes on the pay-off, what Judases often don't see is that the true motivation for betrayal is the deficiency of not knowing that they matter, that they are valuable, and that they are good enough *without* having to sell out innocent people.

You might think or hope that your co-workers appreciate you for all that you bring to the table. But when a Judas looks at a person who is competent, capable and willing to share their gifts, talents, knowledge, skills and abilities, the feelings of deficiency in that Judas usually show up as jealousy and envy of the other person. Judas seldom looks inside of himself or herself. Judas always looks on the outside, looking at what he or she can get. That's why it's so easy for Judas to ignore the fact that betrayal is a seed that hurts. Hurt shows up on the inside, first! But Judas is all about the outside. If Judas could ever get connected with the inside, with heart and soul and spirit, Judas would probably realize that the motivation really *is* all about him or her – not just what they can get, but more about who they are.

You may not have any sympathy or empathy for Judas. And if your world has been rocked by betrayal from Judas, the last thing you probably care about is Judas having low self-esteem. But this is where being an adult and being the mature one comes into play. I'm definitely not suggesting that the fact that your Judas feels like he or she isn't enough is a good reason to betray you. But part of being an adult is being emotionally mature and being able to act like an adult.

People who betray other people are emotionally immature and act like children. They're in pain, kicking and screaming for attention, hurting anyone and everyone who gets in the way of them getting attention. If you're getting attention and accolades because of your good work and because you've got talent, you can expect to get caught in one of Judas' childish tantrums. But adults, that is, *emotionally mature* adults, need to choose the high road. Adults have feelings but they don't allow their feelings to rule them and to motivate them. Adults think things through. Adults don't retaliate and throw tantrums and try to get even. As an adult, you should think this thing through. Mature adults plan before they act. Mature adults think about what they're going to do before they do it. And mature adults think about what the possible consequences of their actions will be.

During the three years that I worked with my Judas and suspected that she was trying to sabotage me, I never allowed her petty ways to change me, to take me out of character or to cause me to deny my integrity. Oh don't get me wrong. I didn't act like we were the best of friends. In fact, I stepped back from her and became what I call "business friendly."

Acting "business friendly" is similar to dressing in "business casual." Business causal means that you don't have to be all suited up. You can dress a bit more casually, but, you keep in mind that the first word is business. In the same way, "business friendly" means you don't have to act like you're meeting someone for the first time and extend them a firm handshake. You can be a bit more relaxed in your conversation, but, you keep in mind that the first word is business.

When I suspected my Administrative Assistant was sabotaging me (but didn't yet have enough evidence to prove it), I became "business friendly." There were no causal lunches. There were no Christmas present exchanges. There were no birthday gifts. I was cordial, but we weren't friends. It was all business. And trust me, my Administrative Assistant absolutely didn't like my "business friendly" approach.

Somewhere during the last year of my employment, my Administrative Assistant still hadn't caught on to the fact that we only worked together, that we weren't friends. So she tried to give me a gift, either for Christmas or for my birthday. But I wasn't about to play her game where she would disrespect me on one day to the point of being insubordinate and then a few days later offer me a gift. When she came to my office with the gift, she tried to hand it to me. But I told her, "No, that's not necessary. You don't have to do that." She was definitely taken aback, and she looked shocked. She took the gift and went back to her desk. But then a few minutes later, just like a child, she stormed into my office, unannounced and uninvited, said that *she* wanted to give me the gift, put it on my desk and then hurriedly exited so that she didn't have to listen to what I might say.

In my opinion, she was acting like a child. She wanted what *she* wanted, just like an immature child. But she didn't realize that she was dealing with an adult – an emotionally mature adult. And as an adult, I decided not to debate and go back and forth with her. I didn't say a word. I finished my workday, took the gift home with me and threw it away. I guess I could have just put the gift in a drawer, left it in the office and not taken it home. But I felt like my

Administrative Assistant's actions were trashy and what she handed me was not a gift but more trash. What better place for the gift than to be with other trash?

In my mind, when I threw the gift away, I was putting an end to the game she was trying to play with me. But in my heart, I knew that my action of throwing the gift away was really because of the pain and anger I was feeling. I was insulted that she would sabotage me on one hand and then glaze over it with a gift on the other hand. In retrospect, I can't say what I did was the action of a mature adult. But throwing the gift away was my way a trying to reclaim and reaffirm my dignity and value as an employee and a person, and to rid myself of feelings of dishonor.

Even after you've been betrayed, you need to act like the adult that you are. You were hired to do a job and you were hired because you're an adult. Don't let Judas' childish antics get in your way and reduce you to his or her level. You may be hurting. But don't be like Judas and get caught up in your feelings. Be the bigger person. Be the person you were hired to be. Be an adult!

STEP 2
REMINDERS

- Emotionally immature people will sabotage people whom they envy.
- Emotionally mature adults manage their feelings and use their brains to think things through before acting.
- People who engage in betrayal have feelings of personal deficiency but they're not always aware of these feelings.

DON'T TAKE IT PERSONALLY!

STEP 3

DO YOUR JOB

❡

While Jesus was going up to Jerusalem, he took
the twelve disciples aside by themselves, and said
to them on the way, "See, we are going up to
Jerusalem, and the Son of Man will be handed
over to the chief priests and scribes, and they will
condemn him to death."

(Matthew 20:17-18)

As they were leaving Jericho, a large crowd
followed him. There were two blind men sitting
by the roadside. When they heard that Jesus was
passing by, they shouted, "Lord, have mercy on us,
Son of David!" The crowd sternly ordered them
to be quiet; but they shouted even more loudly,
"Have mercy on us, Lord, Son of David!" Jesus

stood still and called them, saying, "What do you want me to do for you?" They said to him, "Lord, let our eyes be opened." Moved with compassion, Jesus touched their eyes. Immediately they regained their sight and followed him.

(Matthew 20:29-34)

You're Still on the Clock

In the 1970's, The Steve Miller Band rose to fame with a song titled "Fly Like An Eagle." The guitars, the drums, the organs and the keyboards are all easy. The music is smooth and mellow and makes you feel like you could float away from every care and concern, maybe to a mountain top when the leaves are just starting to change into their fall colors, or to a beautiful breezy beach in the Caribbean with cream- colored sands and turquoise and emerald colored waters.

But then the band starts singing. They imitate the tick-tock sound of a clock and all of a sudden, that carefree feeling gives way to a sense of urgency. The band starts to list all of the things that need to be done in the world. Babies need to be fed. Children need shoes. The homeless need housing. The bottom line is that there's work to do and the tick-tock of the clock says that time isn't standing still.

Midway through the twentieth chapter of Matthew, the writer says that while Jesus and His disciples were traveling across the country, Jesus shared some very interesting information with them. He told them that He would be betrayed and crucified. The remainder of that chapter goes on to say that Jesus facilitated a group discussion on leadership and service, and that He restored sight to two blind men.

In fact, the entire book of Matthew goes on to talk about how Jesus cured the blind and the lame, taught numerous lessons about the Kingdom of Heaven and told what would be the signs of future events. He also answered questions about the resurrection, about taxes, and about the commandments given to the children of Israel by Moses. Jesus did all of this and He was still aware of the very real fact that He was going to be betrayed.

In spite of the future betrayal, Jesus continued to work. He had places to go, people to see and things to do. There were lessons to be taught, diseases to be cured and people to be healed. Jesus wasn't brought on the scene to cower in a corner for fear of what might happen to Him in the future. And He wasn't brought here to pity Himself after the kiss of betrayal was planted on His cheek. There was work that needed to be done and Jesus was the man for the job!

Unlike Jesus, most people don't know when the betrayal is coming. Jesus knew He was going to be betrayed but kept on working. You have to do the same thing. Keep working! You're still on the clock! You can't allow yourself to be distracted from the job at hand. When you become aware of betrayal, you'll have your moments. During those moments, your every waking thought might be consumed by what you have to do now that you've been sabotaged. Damage control may be your top priority. But you can't allow what happened or what might happen to take your focus off the job you were hired to do. When betrayal enters the room, then – more than ever – you need to be on your toes. You need to do your job and do it well!

You've got to Take Care of Business, *YOUR* business, that is. There are certain things that you do well. You have knowledge, skills, abilities, talents and gifts that make you stand out from the crowd. Not everyone who applied for your job was hired. But you were! Now is the time to shine. If Judas is going to strike or has already sucker-punched your professional character, by all means, don't give him or her more ammunition. Regardless of what Judas has managed to damage, there is something left inside of you. "Strengthen what remains!" (Revelation 3:2)

For three years, while my Administrative Assistant was lying on me and conspiring against me, I showed up for work. I showed up physically and I showed up mentally and emotionally. I did the job I was hired to do. Some days were more difficult than others. There were days I dreaded being in the same space as my Judas. Sometimes the tension in the air was so thick it was difficult to remember that somewhere behind the fog, the sun was still shining. But I wasn't in a position, financially, to just walk off the job.

So, during my last year, I applied for other jobs and went on interviews. I even applied for a job with the Supreme Court of Virginia. I made it through two rounds of interviews and had the opportunity to sit down with the Justices of the Supreme Court of Virginia and tell them why I was the best person for the job. In the end, I wasn't hired. I received a letter saying that they had chosen another candidate. But the letter also said how impressed they were with my qualifications and my experience and how much they enjoyed having the opportunity to meet me. It was the most uplifting and empowering rejection letter I had ever received! The Justices of the Supreme Court of Virginia were impressed by *me*.

A few months later I ran into the Chief Justice at a grocery story. He remembered me, told me about other openings with the Court and encouraged me to apply. That gave me hope and reminded me that I had something valuable to offer. Maybe not to the Supreme Court of Virginia, but to someone. And in the meantime, I still had a job, even if it was with the person who was sabotaging me. So I showed up and I did what I was hired to do.

Even if Judas has caused you to lose your job, you still have the knowledge and skills that earned you the job in the first place. Find another job! Start your own business! You're created in the image of the Creator, so create your future! If the betrayal doesn't kill you, allow it to make you *better,* not *bitter!*

People will believe what they want to believe, even if it's a lie. And unfortunately, no matter what you do, some people will continue to believe the lie. Everyone wants to be liked and accepted. And I'm sure your employer wants you to be pleasant and cordial with people. But you're not being paid just for people to like you. You were hired to do a job. You're still on the clock. So do your job!

STEP 3
REMINDERS

- If you're still employed after Judas betrays you, then your job is to continue using the talents that earned you the job.
- If Judas causes you to lose your job, then your job is to use your talents to find another job or become your own boss.
- There is a job that needs to be done and only you can do it.

DO YOUR JOB!

STEP 4

EMBRACE JUDAS' EXPERTISE

Then Jesus summoned his twelve disciples and gave them authority over unclean spirits, to cast them out, and to cure every disease and every sickness.

(Matthew 10:1)

Traitors Have Skills Too

In Matthew 10:1, the writer says that Jesus gave the disciples authority. By giving the disciples authority, He gave them power. If we take the next logical step, after Jesus gave the disciples power, we can assume that they used this power. Here is another fact to consider. As one of the twelve disciples, Judas received authority and power, too. And, he used it!

We may not want to admit it, but Judas had skills. People were healed because of the power which had been given to Judas. The message of the Master was furthered because of Judas. No doubt, Jesus saw Judas' faults and frailties, but He also saw Judas' strengths and skills. And that's what He worked with. He didn't throw the baby out with the bath water.

Like so many people in the bible, Judas left a very negative legacy. When the twelve disciples are named for the first time in the books of Matthew, Mark and Luke, each writer refers to Judas as "the traitor." His deed as a traitor came during the very last days of his life. But for most of his time as a disciple, he served as a productive part of Jesus' team. Christians have a saying, "Love the sinner but hate the sin." That saying suggests that the negative things that a person does are not one and the same as the person. And despite the dirty things that people do, there is often still some good in these people.

You may not want to work with your Judas. You may want him or her to quit or be fired. That may be what you want because you feel that Judas has nothing of value to offer. But as painful as it may be for you to admit it, your Judas has skills and, more than likely, that is why Judas is still working on that job with you.

I can imagine some people might say, "No! Judas' work is horrible and he or she should have been let go a long time ago." Or, maybe you might be saying, "No! Judas should have been let go long ago because Judas doesn't do *any* work." If either of these statements is true and Judas is still employed, then there's probably a person or two who is picking up the slack and doing Judas' job. If this is the case and if you're the person who's constantly picking up the slack, constantly having to do damage control because of a particular co-worker's poor performance, then you should address the issue with management in a professional manner. However, the likelihood is slim to none that a person would perform horribly *all* of the time or not do any work *any* of the time, and still be able to maintain employment.

Unfortunately, people with nasty attitudes are often kept on the team because they're still getting the job done. Most businesses won't continue to employ and pay people who don't ever do the job the right way. And most businesses won't continue to employ people who never do any work at all. In your opinion, the quality and quantity of work that Judas performs may not measure up to your standards. However, the truth remains that Judas may still be employed because he or she has skills.

Most people possess a set of skills that earn them a job and allow them to keep a job. Minus the character flaws and the deficiencies that cause Judas to betray innocent people, Judas, like you, has a job to do and, more than likely, does reasonably well. At a minimum, Judas does the job *well enough.* Whether you hired Judas or whether you work with Judas because of someone else's hiring decision, each of you has parts of the whole. And although you may not agree, there are people on the job who trust Judas to do the part of the job that he or she was hired to do.

If you suspect that there's a Judas on your job or if you *know for sure* that there's a Judas (because the betrayal has already taken place) chances are you may have to continue working with Judas. But don't sell yourself short. You can do this. You'll just need to concentrate on Judas' positive skills instead of Judas' character flaws.

My Administrative Assistant was a Judas and she was busy scheming and lying on me to my supervisor whenever she had a chance. Or she was busy just being passive aggressive toward me. But she also had valuable skills. And as much as I hate to admit it, I couldn't have done my job without her skills. In addition to my having to facilitate training sessions on subjects like sexual harassment awareness and prevention, disabilities and reasonable accommodations, and having to investigate allegations of unlawful discrimination, my office had a steady stream of job announcements that I had to make sure were compliant with hiring practices regarding affirmative action. My Administrative Assistant was skilled when it came to finding just the right websites, journals and other places where the jobs could be advertised. She was a backstabber when it came to me as a person, but when it came to her job, she was on the ball.

Perhaps your Judas is excellent at writing and mailing out all the correspondence that keeps you in touch with your network of associates. Maybe your Judas gets a kick out of filing all day or restocking shelves and clothing racks. Or maybe your Judas loves presenting at meetings that last for endless hours. It could be that your Judas develops wonderful presentations. Or maybe Judas is good at conducting investigations and gathering facts that allow you to write those amazing reports that have earned you wonderful performance evaluations. Maybe Judas is good at doing all the prep work in the background that lets you shine out front. Whatever Judas does, Judas has skills and that's probably why Judas is still working with you.

Judas was still in Jesus' company, even after Jesus made His first announcement that He would be "handed over" to His enemies. Jesus probably wouldn't have kept Judas as a disciple if Judas didn't have skills or if Jesus thought that Judas was just a waste of time and space. Jesus didn't just keep Judas around because he felt sorry for him. Jesus had work to do and Judas was part of that work. Like it or not, even after the kiss of death, you and Judas may still have to work together. Acknowledging that Judas adds value to the job will take a certain level of maturity. But we've already established that you're an adult, right? Judas has skills. So embrace them!

STEP 4
REMINDERS

- Judas was hired because Judas has knowledge and skills that meet a professional need.
- Judas is still on the job because someone in a position of authority believes that Judas adds professional value to the team.
- Focus on the positive contributions that Judas makes to the work that needs to be done instead of focusing on Judas' negative behavior.

**EMBRACE
JUDAS' EXPERTISE!**

CHOOSE YOUR
WORDS WISELY

When it was evening, he took his place with the twelve; and while they were eating, he said, "Truly I tell you, one of you will betray me." And they became greatly distressed and began to say to him one after another, "Surely not I, Lord?" He answered, "The one who has dipped his hand into the bowl with me will betray me. The Son of Man goes as it is written of him, but woe to that one by whom the Son of Man is betrayed! It would have been better for that one not to have been born."

*Judas, who betrayed him, said, "Surely not I,
Rabbi?" He replied, "You have said so."*

(Matthew 26:20-25)

⟩⟨⟩⟨

Talk Therapy

On at least two occasions before Jesus observed the
Passover with His disciples, He mentioned the fact
that He was going to be betrayed. We can assume that
Judas was present both times. During the Passover meal,
Jesus brought it up again, and we know for sure that Judas
was present. According to the scripture, all of the disciples
asked, one at a time, if he was the one who would betray
Jesus. The scripture also records that Judas was the only
one to whom Jesus responded directly.

There's no clear reason given as to why Jesus repeatedly
brought up the betrayal or why He only responded to Judas.
On the other hand, what stands out is that Jesus lets Judas
know that He's very aware of the fact that Judas is going
to betray Him. Judas said, "Are you saying that I'm going
to sell you out?" And Jesus responded, "Your words, not
mine."

One thing I've discovered is that, for any number of reasons, if we see a scheme underway, especially one where we
may be the target, human nature kicks in and we don't want

our betrayer to think that the wool is being pulled over our eyes. Nobody likes to get "got." There's something about us that makes us want to tell Judas, "I see you. And I see what you're doing." Even if we aren't in a position to stop the betrayal, we still want Judas to know that we aren't completely blindsided. And if we aren't in a position to tell Judas directly, "I see you!" inside our heads we're still saying, "I see you!" I believe that's what Jesus said to Judas. When Judas asked, "Am I the one who's going to betray you?", and Jesus responded, "You said it," I believe Jesus was saying, "I see you."

During the time that I was working with my Administrative Assistant, I constantly confronted, counseled and coached her about her professional behavior. And on the last day of my job, we talked about "the betrayal." In fact, she brought up the subject. She said that guilt was eating her up and that she had to confess what she'd done. She said that she had conspired with my supervisor to "create" reasons to sabotage me and get rid of me. In other words, she agreed to tell lies about my job performance.

While she confessed, I sat and I listened. I never asked her what she received in return for betraying me because it didn't matter. She became teary-eyed as she confessed. I didn't try to comfort her. I didn't nod or give any verbal sign that I understood, which was so unlike me because I'm an active listener. But I just sat stolid, looking her straight in her eyes. And in my mind I kept saying to myself, "I *knew* you were scheming! I *knew* you had something to do with me losing my job. *I knew it!*"

She said she was sorry and that she was praying for God to forgive her. But she didn't ask for my forgiveness. And I didn't offer it because at that point I wasn't able to say the words, "I forgive you," and mean them. At that time, I thought that if I had said, "I forgive you," it would have been the same as excusing her bad behavior and would have been a way for her to ease her feelings of guilt. Sitting across from her, every fiber of my being said, "You *should* feel guilty and you need to *sit* in that guilt – *for a while*. No! You don't get an 'I forgive you' from me today." So I sat there and listened to her apology, which I really didn't want or need because I didn't believe she meant it, and because the damage was already done.

However, what I wanted and what I got was confirmation of what I had suspected three months into the job. And that confirmation was that this woman, my Administrative Assistant, was someone who was sneaky and couldn't be trusted. It was my last day on the job. I was happy to be moving on and looking forward to what the future held for me. Since she finally decided to confess to betraying me, I decided that I would have the last word about her betrayal. But the last word for me wasn't that I would give her a piece of my mind. The last word for me was to keep my words to a minimum. I felt that I had the right to not engage in a cathartic conversation for her benefit. I didn't think I was obligated to hold a counseling session and help her work through her guilt. In the same way that I wasn't able to say, "I forgive you," I also wasn't able to play the role of the compassionate counselor. It was time for me to leave. And the last word for me was that I had a right to say as little or as much as I wanted to say. So, after she gave me her confession and apology, I said "Okay. Thank you for telling me." That may sound insincere, but I really meant it. I was thankful to know that I had been right about her all along.

I *knew* she was up to no good and her confession some-how made me feel as if I had won! As I reflect, I hadn't really won anything. Although I was happy to be leaving, I was still without a job and still reeling from the emotional roller coaster I had been on for almost three years. But my ego and my emotions needed vindication, and her confession was the proof that I needed. For me, that was better than an apology. It was enough for me to know that I had seen her true colors. There was not much I wanted to say or needed to say to her. Instead, my last words were, more or less, to myself, and those words were, "I *knew* it!"

I don't feel the need to say everything that comes to my mind. I pick my battles. In fact, I probably only say a fraction of what comes to my mind. And I filter a lot of what I say. During this age of social media, people often verbally abuse and blast each other, for the whole world to read and without giving it a second thought. We live in a very emotionally immature world where people have either not learned or have forgotten how to rationally and calmly talk about problems. Reality shows send a strong message that it's okay to yell and scream and rant and rave when someone hurts your feelings. These shows teach people that you have a right to "throw shade" and even throw punches if someone disrespects you. People end up talking *at* each other instead of talking *to* each other, and nothing ever really gets solved. We live during a time when people are determined to have the last word of the conversation, and the purpose of getting the last word in isn't so that the conflict can be resolved. The purpose is just to have the last word – period!

I believe in talking *to* people, but only when it's appropri-ate. And there are times when, given the occasion and the opportunity, saying what's on your mind is the right thing to do. At the moment when my Administrative Assistant brought up the subject of her betrayal of me, that could have been prime time for me to unload choice words on her. However, I chose to handle it another way. I chose to "hold my peace." Your Judas may not willingly come to you to confess. You may have to make the first move. And if you're one of those people who has a tendency to engage in arguments in your head and carry resentment throughout your life, perhaps, you should have a talk with Judas. *But before you talk to Judas*, there are a couple of things you need to consider.

First, you need to examine your motives. If you're looking for a confession and an apology from Judas, chances are slim to none that you'll get either one. My situation was unique, and I received a confession and an apology. But I never thought the apology was genuine. And years later I learned that the confession was really a way for my Administrative Assistant to turn the knife in my back just a little bit more. It turned out that she had played the same twisted game of betrayal on my predecessor and my successor. And she received some sort of perverted joy by telling me and others what she had done. So as it turns out, neither the confession nor the apology were honest.

Confessions are not one of Judas' strong points. And your chances of getting an apology are even slimmer. You probably shouldn't expect anything in return from Judas except his or her excuses and your frustration, neither of which you will find helpful. But, if you still have to work with Judas after being betrayed by him or her, and if you decide that you need to confront Judas about the betrayal, you should do it discreetly. Some of your co-workers may be aware of what Judas has done to you. But this doesn't mean your *talk* with Judas should be a public one. If you decide to address Judas about the betrayal, do it as privately as possible. And before you speak your piece, you should prepare yourself to not feel hurt or angry when Judas doesn't respond the way you want Judas to respond.

Even if Judas' response doesn't satisfy you, someone else on your job, like your manager or supervisor, may respond favorably to your attempts to correct the situation. On most jobs, being able to discuss problems with the very people or person with whom you have a problem is actually something that many employers view as an attribute. I've had numerous job interviews in which I was asked how I would handle problems with co-workers. My interviewers were looking for specific answers. They wanted to know that I would address my co-worker one on one, with diplomacy and respect. Keep in mind you may still have to work with Judas. The ability to address the person one on one and to address the problem directly are part of team building, and they are signs of a mature adult. (Once again, we've already established that you *are* a mature adult, *and*, that you are going *to be* a mature adult in *this* situation, right?) Employers are looking for people who have good communication and conflict resolution skills, and employers are more likely to keep these people as employees. Therefore, you have to be willing to address the problem and you have to be willing to address the person who caused the problem.

Some people may be hesitant and even opposed to addressing problems with Judas, particularly if there is no likelihood that Judas will apologize. But getting an apology isn't the only reason to talk to Judas. Many people walk around, literally for years, having arguments in their minds because of betrayal. This is no way to live. And even if you aren't re-hashing the issues in your mind, you could easily but unconsciously carry your hurt and anger into your next job if you don't resolve the problem.

Addressing the problem is a step toward letting the problem go. Maybe you want Judas to know that there is a definite line drawn in the sand between what was once a close relationship between the two of you and what is now strictly a business relationship. Or maybe you just want to let Judas know that you were not hoodwinked. Having a talk with Judas is a way to unload that baggage and get some relief. Attempting to resolve the problem with Judas, and relieving yourself of the burden of carrying the hurt of the betrayal are good reasons for having a talk with Judas.

Second, if you decide to talk to Judas, you need to choose your words wisely. As I said earlier, we live during a time when people believe it's acceptable to say exactly what they think and how they feel. Some people spit their words like venom, without a filter, straight up with no chaser! Angry, threatening, hostile words can land you in a number of situations that range from the unemployment line to behind prison bars. Don't think for one second that just because you stop short of hauling off and punching Judas in the face that you don't have to worry about losing your job or your freedom. You need to look before you leap and think before you speak! Andy Rooney, who used to be on the television news show *60 Minutes,* often said, "Keep your words soft and sweet just in case you have to eat them." It's acceptable to express what you feel, but remember, "Death and life are in the power of the tongue," (Proverbs 18:21) and the last thing you want to do is to say something that brings about your own professional death. Make sure your words leave you with life.

Write down what you want to say to Judas and then read it out loud to yourself. Keep it short and sweet. Listen to yourself as you rehearse what you plan to say. You may even want to make a video or an audio recording. If you look and sound angry to yourself, more than likely you'll look and sound angry to Judas, too. Even if you don't think you look or sound angry, you should rehearse your "speech" with a friend who is objective. You don't need friends who will simply co-sign what you feel and what you want to say, regardless of how it sounds and you don't need people to add fuel to the fire. You need an *objective* friend. An objective friend will be able to help you choose non-threatening words to express how you feel and will help you realize when your temper is on the rise.

If you don't have a friend who can help you chose the right words and the right tone, or if you know that you won't be able to stay calm, cool and collected while having your conversation with Judas, it's probably in your best interest to not have the conversation with Judas at all. Instead, you may need to speak with your supervisor, someone else in a management position, or someone in human resources.

Even if you are able to resolve the work-related problems, you may find yourself still seething with anger or hurt over the betrayal, and in need of a listening ear. In that case, talk to a friend, talk to a counselor or therapist, talk to a spiritual advisor, talk to God, talk to yourself! Talking about the betrayal with a trusted person is a way of confronting some of the issues, even if you don't confront Judas. And in essence, by talking about it, you still get to have the last word on how the betrayal affects you.

STEP 5
REMINDERS

- You may need to talk with someone in order to get past the hurt and anger of betrayal.
- If you talk to someone on your job, it should be your supervisor, a manager, an appropriate human resources representative or maybe, even Judas.
- If you talk to Judas, choose your words and your tone carefully so they don't come back to haunt you.

CHOOSE YOUR WORDS WISELY!

PURSUE JUSTICE NOT REVENGE

When Judas, his betrayer, saw that Jesus was condemned, he repented and brought back the thirty pieces of silver to the chief priests and the elders. He said, "I have sinned by betraying innocent blood." But they said, "What is that to us? See to it yourself." Throwing down the pieces of silver in the temple, he departed; and he went and hanged himself.

(Matthew 27:3-5)

You Have a Right to Get Even

After receiving the "kiss of death," Jesus is hauled off to face His accusers, stand trial on trumped-up charges and be crucified. Then suddenly, reality sets in with Judas. The scripture says Judas admitted that he had betrayed an innocent man and he tried to make things right. He thought that if he gave the money back it would undo the deal he had made with the chief priests and elders. But they weren't having any part of it. They basically told him that he was going to have to deal with his guilt by himself.

The story doesn't tell us what motivated Judas to come clean. Some people might argue that his conscience kicked in, and that he felt guilty for engaging in such an underhanded scheme against an innocent man. Others might argue that Judas was merely trying to save himself in case the plan backfired and the authorities and powers-that-be decided to come after him.

Whatever his reason may have been, it's obvious that the guilt Judas felt was too much for him to handle on his own. So he hanged himself, and Jesus had nothing to do with it. In fact, Jesus probably never saw Judas again after the betrayal. But, unlike Jesus, some people will continue to see their Judases after they've been betrayed. And just like there's a natural, human tendency to want Judas to know that we saw the betrayal coming, there's also a natural, human tendency to want to see Judas get what we think he or she deserves. In fact, we might even want to participate in the plan to bring Judas down.

But consider this: Your job description doesn't include revenge or retaliation. Revenge and retaliation won't help you. This doesn't mean that you shouldn't pursue legal recourse if you believe a law has been violated that protects your rights as an employee. By all means, take the proper action to protect your legal rights. But if no laws have been violated that protect your rights and you don't have any type of legal recourse available to you, retaliation is *not* the road to take. There's a saying, "Every time you throw a little dirt, you lose a little ground." Trying to get even and settle the score will only pull you down. And even though you know revenge is not in your best interest, you'll probably still want some type of justice.

After my Administrative Assistant started sabotaging me, I still had to work with her. While going through this period of time, I cried on the shoulders of a few friends. I remember a couple of them trying to comfort me with statements like, "What goes around comes around," and "she'll get hers because you can't mess with God's people." Some of my friends even quoted scriptures like, "touch not my anointed and do my prophet no harm." My friends knew that I wasn't a vengeful person and that I wouldn't try to even the score. But they could feel my pain and they were trying to comfort me by suggesting that God would punish my Judas. But honestly, I didn't find any comfort in their words or in the thought of punishment. That's because I wasn't sure that there would be any type of Providential Payback. I wasn't sure that God would punish my Administrative Assistant for what she had done to me. And to be completely honest, I wasn't concerned about whether she would be punished. My focus wasn't on her. My focus was on me!

Years before I was betrayed, I read in the Bible, "For he says to Moses, I will have mercy on whom I have mercy, and I will have compassion on whom I have compassion. It depends not on human will or exertion, but on God who shows mercy." (Romans 9:15-16)   For many years, these words left me feeling and believing that if there was Divine Justice and punishment to be handed out, it was God's business, not mine. It was up to God as to whether punishment would be extended to my Judas. So I didn't waste my time brooding over whether or not my Administrative Assistant would get what I may have felt she deserved.

One of the more difficult parts of dealing with betrayal is the thought of Judas getting away with the betrayal and never having to pay for what he or she has done. But, going back to what it means to be a mature adult, one of the things you have to accept is that, if punishment is to be handed out, it's not your place to hand it out, and it's not your place to look for it to be handed out. You shouldn't spend your days looking forward to Judas being punished – not because it's an immoral or wrong desire, but because it's a waste of time and energy. Justice belongs to the one who is the Judge.

In the judicial system, there are two parties whenever a case goes to court: a plaintiff and a defendant. The plaintiff is the one who has been harmed or injured. The defendant is the one who is accused of causing the harm or the injury. Neither the plaintiff nor the defendant gets to decide the outcome of the case. Both sides put on their best cases and present the facts as they see them (or as they want them to be seen) but they don't get to decide the verdict. The final and full verdict can only be decided by the judge.

Even when the evidence is heard by a jury, the judge still has a significant role to play in guiding the jury's verdict and determining the punishment.

If or when you are betrayed, you are the plaintiff and your Judas is the defendant. All of the facts may be in your favor, but it's not up to you to say what the final verdict for Judas will be. It's not up to you to issue out punishment or retaliation. That job belongs to the judge. If your employer is the judge, then it's up to the employer to decide what will be done to Judas. And if the employer is blinded by Judas and doesn't find any fault, remember: "The eyes of the Lord are in every place, keeping watch on the evil and the good," (Proverbs 15:3) and God is a righteous judge. If Judas needs to be punished, God can and God will handle it because punishment or "retributive justice" belongs to God.

Justice is like a coin and retribution is only one side of that coin. The other side is restoration. Retributive justice is what Judas sometimes deserves and sometimes gets. Restorative justice is what you deserve and what you can absolutely get. Even if you lose your job because of the betrayal, you can still be restored by getting another job. You don't deserve pity parties or low self-esteem or the distraction of trying to get even. You have too much to offer and you have too much to gain. After you've been betrayed, if you believe you deserve restoration, you're right.

You deserve the opportunity to continue doing the excellent work you've always done, even though the opportunity may be in a different setting. This is the restoration you deserve and this is the side of the coin where your focus needs to be. Someone once said, "Success is the best revenge". So stay focused on your plans and goals and dreams. Focus on your success. Focus on your future. And follow the motto of the First Lady of the United States of America, Michelle Obama: "When they go low, you go high."

The past has something to teach you. So look back at the betrayal, get the best parts that this experience has taught you, and take those lessons with you into your future. Reaching back and gathering the best parts will allow you to achieve your full potential as you move forward. Whatever you've lost or whatever has been taken from you can be replaced, revitalized, and reproduced.

STEP 6
REMINDERS

- Talk to a human resources person or an attorney if you believe your legal rights as an employee have been violated.
- Don't engage in personal revenge or retaliation because it won't help you and it may actually hurt you.
- Punishment is not your business so don't waste your time and energy pursuing it.
- Focus your time and energy on moving forward with your plans, goals, and dreams for the future.

PURSUE JUSTICE NOT REVENGE!

CHECK IN WITH YOUR INNER CIRCLE

—⊰+⊱—

*Now when Jesus came into the district of Caesarea
Philippi, he asked his disciples, "Who do people
say that the Son of Man is?" And they said,
"Some say John the Baptist, others say Elijah,
and still others Jeremiah or one of the prophets."
He said to them, "But who do you say that
I am?" Simon Peter answered, "You are the
Messiah, the Son of the living God."*

(Matthew 16:13-16)

*From that time on, Jesus began to show his
disciples that he must go to Jerusalem and
undergo great suffering at the hands of the elders*

and chief priests and scribes, and be killed, and on the third day be raised.

(Matthew 16:21)

Six days later, Jesus took with him Peter and James and his brother John and led them up a high mountain by themselves.

(Matthew 17:1)

You Are Not Alone

Halfway through Matthew's record of the gospel, Jesus asked His disciples to tell Him what people had been saying about Him. At this point, Jesus had already come in contact with a lot of people and had already preached to hundreds, maybe even thousands. He had cured people who had potentially fatal illnesses, calmed stormy seas, restored sight to the blind and restored health and wholeness to people who had other physical and mental limitations. People had seen and heard enough about Jesus to form an opinion about him. So Jesus asked, "What are the people saying?" The answers and opinions were all over the place and ranged from John the Baptist to the prophets like Elijah or Jeremiah, all of whom were dead! Jesus took it a step further. He asked the disciples what they thought of Him. Jesus asked His co-workers for their opinions of Him and Peter declared that Jesus was the Son of God.

In essence, Peter paid Jesus the highest compliment that could be paid. Not that Jesus was searching for compliments, but the fact that Peter knew exactly who Jesus was probably made Jesus feel a sense of fulfillment and that his teachings had struck home. Not long after this moment, Jesus, the Son of God, shared with his disciples that he was going to suffer and be crucified. The feeling in the room obviously changed and things became a little tense when Jesus had to set Peter straight about his wrong way of thinking. But then, just a few days later, Jesus took James, John and Peter by themselves on a retreat. Jesus knew He was about to face the biggest challenge of His life, which would ultimately end with His death, but He made a point of having some private time with His inner circle.

When you're being sabotaged and betrayed by a co-worker whom you thought you could trust, it's easy to get caught up in your emotions and live in your feelings. It's easy and it's natural for all of your attention to be on watching Judas and reacting to Judas' bad behavior. And even though your Judas may be making you feel miserable on the job, you have an alternative.

There are people around you, people who work with you, who see your value. Some of your co-workers, maybe even most of your co-workers, think you're the best person to come through the doors in a long time. They look to you as an example of leadership. They admire you. In their eyes, you're genuine. There's nothing fake or phony about you. They see you as a person who is serious about the work and, at the same time, as a person who cares about other people. They come to you for answers. You've changed the atmosphere in the office. You've brought integrity and professionalism into the workplace. You need to spend time with *these people.*

Don't give Judas all or even most of your mental or emotional energy. Judas is only one person out of the dozens or even hundreds of people who work with you. Judas' negative attitude and behavior deserves as little attention from you as possible. You may have to work with Judas but you don't have to let him or her live in your head. Don't let Judas distract you from your job or the positive people who surround you. If you do, you run the risk of developing a negative attitude and a toxic personality that bleeds onto other people in the workplace and in your private life. Don't feed Judas' deficiency! Instead, bask in the glow of the admiration you receive from the majority of your co-workers.

Judas' opinion of you is misguided and isn't based in the truth. Soak up those compliments, affirmations and warm fuzzy feelings that you get from positive people. Spend your time with people who make your life *better.*

The people who didn't really know Jesus were stuck in the past, thinking that Jesus was John the Baptist, Elijah or Jeremiah. All of them were dead! Jesus never took His identity from dead declarations that people may have made about Him. He knew that He was the embodiment of life. And Peter knew life when he saw it! Jesus was surrounded by people who came to Him, day in and day out. But He chose to be around a small group, and from this small group, He had an inner circle: Peter, James and John. He chose to spend personal, intimate time with this inner circle. That's what you need to do. While your Judas is busy trying to tear you down, there are decent, generous people in your life and on your job who are busy trying to build you up. Spend your time with them!

For three years, Monday through Friday, for the better part of the day, I worked in the office with my Administrative Assistant ... alone. People were in and out all day but they were only "in" for a few minutes. After they took care of whatever business needed taking care of, they were "out." And I was, once again, alone with the person who I knew was stabbing me in the back. But instead of sitting around and sulking over the bad vibe I was getting from my Judas, I left my office, frequently, to be around supportive people. That was the good thing about my job. I was expected to mix, mingle, network and develop working relationships with everyone, from support staff to heads of departments. I was expected to "make rounds." And while I made my rounds, I made a point of checking in with people who knew what I was going through and who were in my corner. I had a small group of work-friends who kept me sane and gave me a safe space to vent my frustrations. They also gave me a place to forget about the drama that my Administrative Assistant was stirring up. I worked with a lot of people but only developed close relationships with three particular people, and they became my inner circle.

We shared stories about family. We collaborated on special projects. We supported each other through illnesses, new job promotion jitters and new love interests. My inner circle reminded me that there was life outside of and apart from my Judas. They made one of the worse times in my professional life bearable and, at times, pleasant. I had to work with my betrayer, but I chose to spend time with my friends.

If you chose to spend time with co-workers, spend time with that small inner circle of people who are supportive of you. Spend time with two or three co-workers who are positive and professional. Minimize your time with negative people like Judas and maximize your time with positive co-workers. Judas is only one bad apple. Ignore the one bad apple and redirect your attention to your co-workers who haven't been infected by Judas' bad behavior. You have a bunch of people in your corner. Don't allow one bad apple to spoil everything for you.

STEP 7
REMINDERS

- Your job is just one part of your life, not your whole life.
- Take advantage of opportunities to be around positive people at work and away from work.
- Identify two or three co-workers or friends who will support you professionally and personally.
- Be intentional about receiving, as well as giving, support to the people in your inner circle.

CHECK IN WITH YOUR INNER CIRCLE!

FORGIVE YOUR FRIENDS

✦

*Then Jesus said to them, "You will all become
deserters because of me this night; for it is written,
'I will strike the shepherd, and the sheep of the
flock will be scattered.' But after I am raised up,
I will go ahead of you to Galilee." Peter said to
him, "Though all become deserters because of you,
I will never desert you." Jesus said to him, "Truly
I tell you, this very night, before the cock crows,
you will deny me three times." Peter said to him,
"Even though I must die with you, I will not deny
you." And so said all the disciples.*

(Matthew 26:31-35)

After a little while the bystanders came up and said to Peter, "Certainly you are also one of them, for your accent betrays you." Then he began to curse, and he swore an oath, "I do not know the man!"

(Matthew 26:73-74)

This Is Your Race

The last days of Jesus' life moved quickly. During the last twenty-four hours of His life, Jesus' body was anointed for burial (while He was still living) by the woman with the box of perfume, and Judas made his deal with the chief priests. But that wasn't all that happened in those twenty-four hours. Jesus ate the Passover meal with His disciples, and He told them that one of them would betray Him. He introduced a memorial meal for the disciples to observe after His death. He told the disciples that all of them would desert Him. He revealed that Peter would deny Him three times. He went to Gethsemane, and prayed and pleaded for God to spare His life. He was betrayed by Judas, violently arrested, and put on trial before the high priest. And finally, He was sentenced to death and denied by Peter. That was a lot to go through in one day. I'm sure Jesus could have used some support. He could have used a friend, perhaps the disciples or maybe someone from his inner circle, like Peter.

Peter would have been the perfect person to support Jesus during this terrible time. The writers of Matthew, Mark and Luke said that Peter was the first person that Jesus called to be a disciple. Undoubtedly, Peter had been with Jesus from the beginning.

Jesus had been a guest in Peter's home. When everyone else was saying that Jesus was John the Baptist, Elijah, Jeremiah or one of the prophets, all of whom were dead, Peter was the one who said that Jesus was the Christ, the one who was alive and who was sent to give life! Peter was the one who had regular conversations with Jesus. He reminded Jesus that he and the other disciples had left everything to follow Him and they needed to know what they would get in return. Peter was the one who asked Jesus how many times he should forgive his brother who constantly hurt him. Peter was one of the three hand-picked by Jesus to go on a private mountain retreat, and Peter was the one who said it was good for them to be on that mountain. It was Peter who spoke up on behalf of all the disciples and asked Jesus to explain to them what it meant for a person to be unclean. And it was Peter who made a vow to Jesus that he would always stand by Him. In fact, it was Peter who told Jesus that he would die with Him before he turned his back on Him.

Peter was definitely Jesus' "ride or die" partner. That is, until it was actually time for Jesus to die. Not only did Peter not stand by Jesus and die with him, Peter completely denied knowing Him! And yet, after Jesus' death, resurrection and appearance to the disciples (before He ascended to Heaven), it was Peter who was the first and strongest supporter to carry on the work that Jesus started. It would have been great if Peter had stood with Jesus and not denied knowing him. But in the end, Peter did what all people do. He went as far as he could.

There's a place in the road where your supporters will stop walking and you'll have to go the rest of the way by yourself. This doesn't mean they're not still in your corner. They are! They want you to get over this hurdle of betrayal and they're still cheering for you. The difference is that they may be cheering you on from a different place or in a different way. They haven't abandoned you. They've just gone as far as they can go. This is your race. Don't expect them to run it for you. Your co-workers and friends' job is to support you, not be a substitute for you.

As wonderful as your co-workers think you are and as much as your friends and family love you, they won't ever feel exactly what you feel. They may have sympathy for you. They may say they feel your pain, but it may not be as intensely as you feel it. And as close as you may be with them, they're not required to live in the pain with you. If they do, that's great! But if they don't, go easy on them.

Your co-workers have their own work to do. They're probably doing as much for you as they can. And they may even feel torn between sympathizing with and supporting you, and trying to remain objective while doing their own work. When your co-workers aren't able to give you exactly what you need during those tough times when you're dealing with Judas, go easy on them. They can't neglect their responsibilities and spend all of their time battling Judas. Neither can your friends and family.

Your friends have their own lives to live. It doesn't make them bad friends or bad people if they aren't able to spend as much time with you as you'd like. Your friends know you're hurting, especially if they're part of your inner circle. But even friends have a right to step back so that they can take care of themselves and their own business. It's called self-preservation, and self-preservation in itself isn't a bad thing. When your friends aren't physically available to help you during your times of struggle, it doesn't mean they've denied you. The same applies to family members, especially if it's a family member contributing to the household where you live.

Managing the stress of betrayal can be consuming. There may be days when Judas is all you can think about, and you're distracted from cooking or cleaning or doing whatever needs to be done to make sure your home is still running smoothly. On those days, when you're consumed with the betrayal, if there are other responsible adults in your home, you can't demand that they ignore household responsibilities, and give all of their time to soothe and counsel you. And if you do make this demand of them, you can't expect that everything else that needs to be done in the house will somehow get done. Even when you're at wits' end, someone has to hold things together. Everyone can't fall apart.

Someone has to pay household bills. Someone has to cook or buy food. Someone has to wash clothes. Taking care of the house and everything that goes with it doesn't mean that your family doesn't care about you. If you're consumed with your Judas drama and you're not able to do things that you normally do around the house, the fact that your family members are stepping up and stepping in to do those things is a clear sign that your family is still in your corner.

Everyone wants to be affirmed, but affirmation comes in different ways. Just because affirmation doesn't come the way that you want it to come doesn't mean that you've been denied by your family. So don't take it personally. And don't take it personally if they disagree with you on some things or have a different opinion from the one that you have, especially when it comes to your Judas issues. A difference in opinion doesn't mean they've abandoned you. I had to come to terms with this truth when I was dealing with my Judas.

When I first noticed that I was being disrespected on my job, I thought my director/supervisor was stirring up trouble. I thought she was turning the office staff, primarily my Administrative Assistant, against me. My supervisor was a white woman and I was sure that she was discriminating against me because I'm an African American woman.

While I was going through this ordeal, one of my cousins came to visit me for about a month. I remember telling her husband that I thought I was being discriminated against by my supervisor and he asked, "But why would she do that?" I felt like he'd slapped me in my face. He had asked me a rational question when, in my mind, he wasn't supposed to ask a rational question. In my mind and my emotions, he was supposed to just feel my pain and be on my side. He wasn't supposed to try to make sense of, or understand, why my supervisor would discriminate against me. He was just supposed to agree with me.

I was so wrong! As distraught and upset as I felt, my cousin wasn't obligated to be in my feelings with me. He had a right to be rational. And he had a right to try and understand the irrational behavior of discrimination. He wasn't denying what I felt, and he wasn't leaving me in the race by myself. He was just trying to understand so that he could support me in the best way possible. I'm glad I didn't let my feelings get the best of me that day.

This is what you need to keep in mind. You have people in your corner who will support you while you're dealing with this ordeal of betrayal. But your supporters can only do so much for you. And they can only go so far with you. The co-workers who support you should be professional and helpful. The friends and family who support you should be kind, polite and compassionate. But you're the one who Judas has betrayed. This is your race. Don't expect your co-workers, friends and family to run it for you. That's just not a realistic expectation. And when your co-workers, friends and family take a break or have a different perspective, don't judge them. And don't cut them out of your life.

STEP 8
REMINDERS

- You have co-workers, friends and family members supporting you while you're dealing with Judas' betrayal.
- People can support and affirm you in ways that aren't directly related to the Judas drama.
- When your supporters take a break from the Judas drama, they aren't abandoning you.
- Your supporters need time to take care of themselves and their business.

FORGIVE YOUR FRIENDS!

STEP 9

SAY YOUR PRAYERS

Then Jesus went with them to a place called Gethsemane; and he said to his disciples, "Sit here while I go over there and pray." He took with him Peter and the two sons of Zebedee, and began to be grieved and agitated. Then he said to them, "I am deeply grieved, even to death; remain here, and stay awake with me." And going a little farther, he threw himself on the ground and prayed, "My Father, if it is possible, let this cup pass from me; yet not what I want but what you want."

(Matthew 26:36-39)

It's Time to Call on a Higher Power

It seems that the end of Jesus' life was near. For three years, Jesus had worked with someone whom He knew was going to eventually betray Him. He knew it was Judas because He had been paying attention to everyone and everything around Him. He knew Judas was the one most likely to betray Him because they had worked so closely together and Jesus had gotten to know Judas' character and personality. In spite of knowing that He was going to be betrayed, Jesus kept doing His job and He did it well! He kept preaching messages and teaching lessons that changed people's lives. He kept healing people from deadly diseases and even raised dead people back to life. He was going to be betrayed. He knew this. But He never stopped working.

Not only did Jesus keep doing His job, He kept working with Judas. Judas may have had some character flaws and personality deficiencies, but he also had some useful skills. So Jesus kept him on the team and continued working with him. And when times were really hard, Jesus had an inner circle, two or three close friends, with whom He could spend private, quality time.

Jesus had worked with the same twelve men for the last three years. But now, it was midnight and Jesus was by himself. He was about to be betrayed by one of His closest colleagues, convicted of crimes He didn't commit, and hanged on a cross to die! Now was the time that He turned to His inner circle, Peter, James and John. But they fell asleep on Him! It was midnight, and at midnight, problems always seem bigger. Abandoned, betrayed, and facing certain death, Jesus did the only and last thing He could possibly do. He prayed!

Jesus knew what He was facing but it didn't mean He was looking forward to it. He wasn't! He didn't want to suffer. He didn't want to be rejected. He didn't want to be tortured. He didn't want to die. His disciples and His inner circle couldn't help Him. So He decided to consult a higher power and pray for a different outcome. He didn't know if it would help, but it certainly couldn't hurt. So He prayed and He prayed and He prayed some more. And an hour later, He got up from His knees, dried His tears and went on to meet His destiny. He didn't get what He wanted, but He got what He needed. What He wanted was to escape betrayal, torture and death. What He got was strength to complete the job He was sent to do.

I had some really good friends and wonderful people in my life who supported me. But when I was dealing with the Judas on my job, at the end of each day when I went home, I was alone. I had a lot of time to think. I had a lot of time to talk to myself. And I had a lot of time to talk to God, *my* higher power. I went back and forth with God for almost three years trying to understand what was going on. I didn't ask, "Why me?" but I did ask, "Why?" And for every "why" that I thought I had identified, I tried to find a way to fix it.

I had a meeting with the Executive Vice President of my organization and I tried to negotiate a way to continue working for the employer. At that point, I really didn't want to stay, but I needed an income. So I was willing to stay for the sake of the money. But my negotiations failed.

I met with other administrators and tried to convince them that I was being unlawfully discriminated against by my supervisor. But no one seemed to see the discrimination except for me. Of course, I later found out that my supervisor wasn't the culprit. It was my Administrative Assistant feeding my supervisor lies about me. As my last days on the job grew closer and closer, my heart sank deeper and deeper, and my despair grew more and more.

I was at the end of my rope and I went into a serious depression. I cried all of the time, at the drop of a hat. I was tired of crying and I wanted and needed relief. I'm somewhat of a "teetotaler". In other words, I'm not big on drinking alcohol. But at one point during this ordeal with my Administrative Assistant, on Fridays I would buy a bottle of wine and a pizza, go home and self-medicate my pain. I did this for about one month until I came to my senses and realized this wasn't the best or the healthiest way for me to deal with my pain, and that I was developing a really bad habit. Plus, I really didn't like the taste of the wine. So my weekly bottle of wine and a whole pizza was marked off my list of quick-fixes.

Instead, I made an appointment with my doctor and she prescribed an anti-depressant medication for me. The medication definitely took the edge off my overwhelming feelings of sadness. But it took the edge off my feelings too much. Not only was I not sad anymore, but I also didn't feel joy, or any kind of emotion. I was just numb, and I didn't like being numb. So I only took the anti-depressants for a few months.

I was still going back and forth with God. But there finally came a point when I stopped going back and forth and

I turned to God, completely. With nobody but my higher power, my God, I cried and I cried and I cried some more. And I prayed and I prayed and I prayed some more. I didn't ask God to change the situation. The decision had already been made that my job was going to end on October 31. My focus was on the future. And I needed a job on November 1, or very shortly thereafter. So that's what I prayed about. I prayed that one of the job applications I had submitted would earn me an interview. And I prayed that one of the interviews would earn me a job. I prayed about the future. And I cried about the pain I was feeling in the present.

For almost three years I had looked around to my family and friends for help. I had looked within myself for help. And then finally, I looked up to my higher power and I prayed for God to help me. Plain and simple, I just needed God's help.

Two weeks before my last day on the job, I got a job offer. It was only a part-time job, tutoring elementary school students in reading and math. It would only last until the end of the school year. And it only paid $14.00 an hour, *well below* what I had been earning as a Deputy Director. So I would have to dip—or more likely, *dive*—into my retirement account. It was only a piece of a job. But something was better than nothing. And this something was just the something I needed after the three years of betrayal and disrespect I had endured.

Every day, when I walked into the classroom to work with those tiny little second graders, they would run to me, hug me and take me by my hand. They ALL wanted "Ms. Adkins" to sit with them. I was hired to work with the students who were struggling with math and reading. But even the star students "loved on" me and wanted my help. Some of them needed my help and some wanted my help. But I needed their help, too. Those second graders gave me much more than the few dollars my paycheck could ever give me. They gave me structure and purpose, peace and appreciation. I had prayed to my higher power for help and that's exactly what I got.

At some point, you have to realize that some things are out of your control. People whom you've worked with for years, whom you thought you could trust, will betray you and you won't be able to stop them. People who've been in your corner to help and support you will suddenly be busy taking care of their own lives. They won't be available and you won't be able to reach them. And all of the strength and courage you had will be gone. Then, more than ever, you need to pray. You need to consult a higher power.

Consulting a higher power isn't about a religion. You don't have to be part of a particular religious denomination. You don't even have to be religious. You don't have to go to church, mosque, temple or any other house of faith in order to acknowledge that you've done all you can do and that you now need help from "Somebody Bigger Than You And I." If you're a person who doesn't ascribe to a particular faith or religious belief, you'll need to decide who or what is your higher power, your source of strength when your own strength is gone, and your source of comfort when your world is falling apart. Drugs, food, alcohol, sex, gambling, excessive shopping, binge watching television and internet shows and movies, and any other activity that you can possibly think of doing isn't the answer. All of these activities are *lower* powers. You need a *higher* power.

If you've *ever* prayed, now is not the time to stop. In fact, you might want to step it up. And if you've *never* prayed, now might be a good time to start. It's great to have other people praying for you. That's one of the ways that your friends and family can show their support for you. But their prayers won't ever be a substitute for your own prayers. In those lonely, midnight hours when you're having one of those dark, heavy moments because your Judas has betrayed you and the worst of it is about to fall on you, your family and friends may be asleep. And trust me, you don't have time to wait for them to wake up and pray for you. You need to pray for yourself.

You don't need a particular formula to pray. Just start talking to your higher power. Talk about your pain, talk about your confusion, talk about your anger, talk about your frustration, talk about your fears. Don't be afraid to pour out your heart and let your tears flow. And don't be afraid to ask for what you want. That's what Jesus did, isn't it? He asked for what He wanted, but He was open to accepting something different.

So go ahead! Ask for what you want. You may get it. But be open to accepting something different, because that "something different" could be just what you need. It may not be comparable to what you had and in some respects it may cause you to have less. Less money, less prestige, less popularity ... LESS! But in other ways, it may cause you to have more. More peace, more joy, more clarity, more focus. The result of praying doesn't mean you'll get what you ask for. When you lose or don't get what you've asked for, there is something better in store for you. But better doesn't mean bigger. Better means what is right for you. And ultimately, getting what is right for you is the best answer to your prayers.

STEP 9
REMINDERS

- Even though you have support *around* you, and resources *inside* you, some things can only be handled by a higher power *above* you.
- What you want may not be what you need.
- Pray for what you want, remain open to receiving what you need, and trust your higher power to give you what is right for you.

SAY YOUR PRAYERS!

Made in the USA
Middletown, DE
02 September 2017